For Mom & Dad
From Mike & Marily—
Christmas 1993

Minnesota Gothic

D1278736

SEEING *DOUBLE* SERIES OF COLLABORATIVE BOOKS

MINNESOTA GOTHIC

Poems by Mark Vinz

Photographs by Wayne Gudmundson

MILKWEED EDITIONS

Minnesota Gothic

Printed in Canada
Published in 1992 by Milkweed Editions.

Milkweed Editions
528 Hennepin Avenue, Suite 505
Minneapolis, Minnesota 55403
Books may be ordered from the above address.

ISBN 0-915943-84-0

95 94 93 92   4 3 2 1

We are grateful for the generous sponsorship of *Minnesota Gothic* by the James R. Thorpe Foundation.

Publication of this book is made possible by grant support from the Literature Program of the National Endowment for the Arts, the Cowles Media / Star Tribune Foundation, the Dayton Hudson Foundation for Dayton's and Target Stores, Ecolab Foundation, the First Bank System Foundation, the General Mills Foundation, the I. A. O'Shaughnessy Foundation, the Jerome Foundation, The McKnight Foundation, the Andrew W. Mellon Foundation, the Minnesota State Arts Board through an appropriation by the Minnesota Legislature, the Northwest Area Foundation, and by the support of generous individuals.

Library of Congress Cataloging-in-Publication Data

Vinz, Mark.
    Minnesota gothic / poems by Mark Vinz ; photographs by Wayne Gudmundson.
        p. cm. — (Seeing double series of collaborative books)
    ISBN 0-915943-84-0 (pbk.)
    1. Minnesota—Poetry. 2. Minnesota—Pictorial works.
    I. Gudmundson, Wayne. II. Title. III. Series: Seeing double.
    PS3572.I58M56 1992
    811'.54—dc20   92-4371
                                                    CIP

"It can hit a hundred and five in July, and forty-five below in January. One hundred and fifty degrees of temperature is how we keep the riffraff out. When that doesn't do it, then it's up to the mosquitoes and leeches. If it wasn't for them, and another thing or two, this piece of God's country would be overrun with people."

—John Day, quoted in *Blue Highways*
by William Least Heat-Moon

For our families and friends—
out there in God's country
hanging on

Poet's Acknowledgments

Many of the poems in this collection have been previously published in the following, sometimes in slightly different form:

Black Willow, Dacotah Territory, Dickinson Review, Elkhorn Review, Gray's Sporting Journal, Great Lakes Review, Great River Review, Image, The Little Magazine, Minnesota English Journal, North Dakota Quarterly, Northern Review, Poetry Now, Poets of the Red River, The Small Farm, South Dakota Review, Sou'wester, Spoon River Quarterly, Studio One, West Branch, and *The Windflower Home Almanac of Poetry.*

"Shooting Signs" first appeared in *Stirring the Deep: The Poetry of Mark Vinz,* ed. Thom Tammaro (Spoon River Poetry Press); "Ritual," "Red River Blues," and "Still Life with Thermometer" also appeared in the chapbook collection *Red River Blues* by Mark Vinz; "In a Drought Year" also appeared in *Climbing the Stairs* (Spoon River Poetry Press) by Mark Vinz; "North of North" also appeared in *Mixed Blessings* (Spoon River Poetry Press) by Mark Vinz; "Two Rivers," © *Minnesota Monthly* magazine, 1986, reprinted with permission of *Minnesota Monthly.*

Special thanks to Dave Wallace for his early help in physically preparing the manuscript; to Bill Holm for his continuing encouragement; to Thom Tammaro, who edited the original version of *Minnesota Gothic* and whose presence is felt in many of these poems; to Wayne Gudmundson, who always helps me to *see*; and, of course, to Betsy, who has helped me in more ways than I can name.

Thanks also to Moorhead State University for a sabbatical leave, during which time final manuscript revisions were completed.

Good Mileage

Photographer's Acknowledgments

Some years ago a friend said, "You know, you're kind of funny." I took it to mean that some of the things I said were funny. He continued, "Yet, I see little evidence of that in your work." In part these photographs are a response to that statement.

About that time Mark Vinz and I were teaching photography and poetry to fourth graders. Our encouraging the students to consider the similarities between the two media began to open my eyes to a certain way of seeing and thinking not only about my work but about Mark's as well.

We seldom responded directly to an image made by the other; rather, we worked in a parallel fashion — framing similar windows on life in a fictitious Minnesota.

I want to thank Frank Gohlke for pointing me in that direction and Mark Vinz for riding along and making the back roads richer.

I also want to acknowledge the generous support of Moorhead State University, the Moorhead State University Foundation, and the Moorhead State University Alumni Association for their assistance in the production of the cover photograph and the accompanying traveling exhibit.

Many of the photographs in this book first appeared on the walls of Ralph's Bar in Moorhead, Minnesota, one dark, cold January evening in 1981.

Girls at the Beach

MINNESOTA GOTHIC

MINNESOTA GOTHIC

GOING HOME

Preface

Collaborations can take many forms, uniting many different media, but there seems to be a particular correlation between the poetic and the photographic image. If both the photograph and the poem depend on angles (and sometimes very unusual ones), both poet and photographer continually ask us to see: to look and look again, and ultimately to open the eyes of our imaginations.

It's exactly in that spirit that Wayne and I worked together for a number of years in the late '70s and early '80s at Fargo's Creative Arts Studio, helping elementary students to see with pinhole cameras and eventually with 35-mm cameras, while at the same time extending the process through the images they could generate with pencil and paper. Just as those students did, we both came to realize important affinities—the ways the poem could be matched to or even generated by the photograph, and vice versa. The two of us went on to collaborate on two broadsides, the first a poem inspired by one of Wayne's photos published in a magazine, the second a photo Wayne matched to one of my poems—as if it were the very image I'd had in mind all along.

Since that time, Wayne has read poems to his university photography classes, as I have shown photos and slides to my literature and writing students. When I've needed photographs for books of my own poems or those I've edited for Dacotah Territory Press, Wayne is the first one I call on, and as recently as a few months ago when Wayne decided he'd like a poem to serve as a preface for a book of photographs by his advanced students, we discovered one of mine that seemed to have been written for the very occasion.

Another affinity we've discovered has something else to do with the angles so essential to our individual work, an idiosyncratic way we each view the world in general and our immediate environment in particular. It involves a shared sense of humor, perhaps, a sense of oddness, a sense of metaphor— it's very hard to define. I call it "Minnesota Gothic," and nowhere else have I seen it as clearly or surprisingly as in Wayne's photographs such as "Reclining Nude" or "Minnesota Fishermen." Indeed, of the latter photograph, I knew from the first time I saw it that someday it would have to be matched with one of my poems, perhaps even become a book cover. It's no surprise to either of us that, at long last, this has happened!

It is in that spirit, finally, that Wayne has found photos to link to many of my poems—not as illustration in any direct sense, but on the ground of those odd and metaphoric angles that are so very important to us both. Certainly, some of the poems in this collaboration (such as "Once Upon A Time") have been directly generated by Wayne's photographs, but even when the affinity has been discovered at a greater distance, those images always seem in some way to have been there in my own work all along. That, I believe, is the most exciting kind of collaboration, and that is what we both hope we've captured in *Minnesota Gothic*.

—Mark Vinz

Outstate

"... it wouldn't be such a bad place to go back to and die in."

—Bob Dylan, quoted in
Growing Up in Minnesota

Big Chief Coffee Shop

She whips the mop around the chairs
and eyes the travelers in the corner booth
picking hairs from their refried corn,
the chicken pale and brittle green.

They call this place a town—
if God knows why, she doesn't.
The trains don't stop here anymore.
A bashed-in windshield is enough
to keep the local boys amazed for hours.

Counter stools revolve like wheels.
Slow today. Nothing but leftovers.
She spears another guest check
flourishes small change into the drawer.
Nearly 20 miles to the Interstate.
Who'd ever claim to be from here?

EAT

Lost and Found

In the small cafe just off the Interstate
they've taken down the photo of the local boy
who pitched in the big leagues for awhile.
Tired farmers visit back and forth
among the table tops and wives—
their round wives with flat accents,
high hair and deep laughs.
The special today is country roasted ham
with corn and bread and American fries.
What was his name, anyway—
the kid from here who used to be a star?
We'll never see another one like that.

Interstate

Gas Station Man: Winter without Snow

As if we don't have enough to worry about,
he says, looking for
a clean spot to wipe his hands.
Think about those fields that never got covered.
That's what I like about the Midwest—
get all psyched up for a good blizzard
and it never happens. Puts everyone on edge.
Just you wait, he says, squinting over
the top of his glasses at the gas pump
he was sure would register more. Just you wait,
we're in for one hell of a spring.

Gas Station

Norwegian Joke

Rodney Sonnegaard backed over
my mailbox one night last week—
took him three tries to knock it down,
three more to trap it with his wheels.

Some people polka,
Rodney flattens mailboxes—
his way of telling us
he's waited all his life
for someone to call him
a sly rascal just once.

Poor Rodney—I watched it all
from my living room window.
The joke's on him this time—
he still thinks I wasn't home!

Can You Believe It?

—for Dave Etter

Once in awhile
one of the local boys
goes plumb nuts.

No way to explain it—
not the moon, not the dust,
not even the humidity.

It just happens.
One day he's normal,
the next he's off

in the fields,
talking to combines
or worse yet, writing down poems—

telling us about apples
like we'd never *seen* apples.
Can you believe it?

Like my wife keeps saying,
some things we're just meant to live with.
Some things can't be figured out.

Come to think of it,
that old woman's been acting
a little strange herself lately.

Tin Can Tower

He drives an 18-wheeler from the coast
and comes this way to save some time—
another wide spot in a bad stretch of road,
just like the place he's from.

He smiles at the railroad crossing
at the edge of town, where sunflowers
have sprouted up between the ties.
One more place to put behind—

Even the CB chatter fades to nothing.
Find a country station on the dial
so the whole cab rings with steel guitars.
Blast the horn to let them know you're here.

Fat crows dive from phone lines,
like something he needs to forget.
Keep it floored. Dakota line by dark,
with nothing but the open road ahead.

Travel-On Motel

They built it years ago
when rumor had it that the Interstate
would come within a mile.
So there it sits at the edge of town—
sentinel in pale pink cinder blocks.

That's her touch. His is the
God Bless America billboard in the drive.
This country's growing and the price
of crops is bound to rise again.
Business will pick up, you know.

Along Highway 12

Mini-Mall

Americana

Once Upon a Time

May sweeps in
across the gentle hills,
over the locust husks of threshing rigs
and workshirts flapping on a sagging line.
In every town a sign
for antiques and collectables.

Somewhere near Dassel
an old man guards a 12-foot ball of string,
fretting over rain and vandals.
Someday he'll built a shed to cover it . . .

Storm clouds to the west.
Beyond the gingerbread houses,
glassed-in cases of barbed wire
and china dolls, rows of hubcaps
nailed to peeling walls,
the old man waits for rain and reporters.
Workshirts flapping on a sagging line.

Ball of Twine

Shooting Signs

Just once I'd like to drive
a stretch in northern Minnesota
and find road signs with
no bullet holes in them.
I've never met anyone who
admitted to shooting signs.
Abandoned farmhouses, that's
another matter, though I've heard
it's mostly kids with shotguns
getting back at parents
for all those years of table manners—
the same way, my friend Keith
tells me, loud tailpipes are
teenagers farting in public.
But who shoots those signs?

Let's fill the woods with signs—
stop signs, yield signs, curve signs,
Men Working signs, and of course
the ones with leaping deer.
Then, let those hunters go
to the woods and shoot their fill—
signs or each other, nothing else.
Think of all the people who could
live off making signs, designing signs,
managing and maintaining signs!
Think of you and me, a hot afternoon
when things aren't going well
at the office—we grab our 30-30s,
jump in the pickup truck, head
to the woods for some shooting,
for some serious fun, you bet!

The Silver Dollar Bar

—for the poets at Southwest State

Everyone orders Schells, the beer
they still brew over in New Ulm,
and why not—this is Ghent,
Minnesota, population 293,
and business is slow this afternoon—
spring plowing and planting furious
against the rage of late May winds.

From the southwest, a line of
thunderheads—be here soon enough,
the old farmer says, and scrubs his hand
along the close-cropped furrows of his head.
This is the place where afternoons
have been known to last for years,
where farmers and poets sip their Schells
and dream themselves back to 1934.

Prohibition through at last, this is
the first bar in the state to re-open.
A camera clicks. Come see us—
not far from Green Valley and Cottonwood,
you can't miss the place—just follow
the dusty winds all the way to the
elevator, turn at the Legion Hall.
You'll know it when you're here.

Gone Fishing

"It is a great blessing, perhaps the
greatest blessing a writer can have,
to find at home what others have to go
elsewhere seeking."

—Flannery O'Connor,
from *Mystery and Manners*

Opener

—for the Lake Blanche crew

They're already scattered—early spawn this year,
shifting cold fronts, last night's lightning,
a threat of storms all day.
We watch the other boats patrolling
shallow, deep, all points between—
like a task force they work,
rechecking read-outs, faces, maps,
and then, far down the shoreline where nobody is,
something flashes silver in deep reeds.

Cut the motor, drift,
fling out the lines and settle back—
something's out there, who knows where?
We fish between the tricky winds
and roiling clouds, rubbing our eyes,
rubbing our backs against
the long dark months of winter sleep.

The Way Home

"Fishermen
Out there,
Casting beyond themselves."
—Thom Tammaro

Hopeless as drunkards
we finally notice lights along the shore.
It's nearly time to head in—
the clouds of bugs, the aching backs,
the fathers we imagine waiting on the dock.
Once again we'll bring back
more poems than fish.

Only a few minutes of light,
and one more strike, perhaps—
the one we've been waiting for
as we troll beside the last reed beds.
And then it won't matter whose line it is
that sings out into dark water.
It won't matter at all.

Getting Away from It All

They like to get away each spring
for a three-day fishing trip—
longer, if the weather holds, if the price
the wives and kids will make them pay
is not too much. You know how it goes.

Under icy stars they pitch their tents.
It's great to be out here alone
together, passing the bottle
and telling all the old familiar lies,
talking about nothing much at all—
not why they came or
what they really left behind,
or even how they feel when
sudden breezes rustle leaves
and something deep within.

Tomorrow will come early—
fish to be caught and cleaned and fried,
cards to be played, and all those
stories to be passed round and round
again. You know how it goes.

Minnesota Fishermen

Photo from an Album Never Kept

Here we have a snapshot of a man
presenting to the camera, with two hands,
a twelve-pound northern pike.
Notice how he's pushed it closer to the lens
so it seems bigger than it is.
Notice, too, his eyes—shy and tentative,
as if this picture and this fish are
things he doesn't really understand,
this ritual of holding onto something dead,
and how there must be millions like it—
someone like someone you've probably met,
trying hard to be proud and bold
about a kind of gift he doesn't know
just whom, or how, to give.

The Forecast

Last night, the TV weather ominous—
high winds with likely snow.
The weatherman recites his grim percentages
with pride—he knows he has us,
that bad weather is more interesting
than none at all.

This morning, sunlight shakes me
like a hand—blue sky and bright.
I rise before the house begins to stir,
to sit and watch a day when
all things seem possible, clear.

It's spring at last, another night survived,
I don't yet drink alone
except for coffee, strong and black
but not too much—
the way my father drank coffee.

My father: gone.
What was it I wanted him to be?
A fisherman who'd teach me secrets
gliding through the shallows
where bass are stirring under lily pads
as gaudy sunlight breaks through pines—

and low clouds scud through my windows
on a rising, chilly wind.
The weatherman returns in polyester plaid:
you see, he tells me, snow is moving in
just as I said it would.

I fish alone—
where lines get tangled in deep weeds.
Tomorrow will be crisp and blue again,
one day closer to season opener.
Today, the snowflakes gather on window sills,
across bedsheets, in every corner of the house.

Snow on Dock

Finding the Big Ones

"All poems are love poems"
—Raymond Carver

The local oracle tilts back his brew—
you've got to know the lake, he says.
The big bass are in the cabbage weed
and thick coontail—use sucker minnows,
the fat ones; forget that plastic crap.

The room is full of nods, our best
aficionado smiles—which also say
we know already nothing much will happen,
that it's always something more
than the right place, the right bait.
And back in the car we have to
speculate again just what went wrong
this time. Fishermen, so full of love
we hardly remember the way home.

Big Fish

Nightfishing

"...unless you are at home in the metaphor, unless you
have had your proper poetical education in the metaphor,
you are not safe anywhere."
—Robert Frost

You're out at night with a small seine,
trying to find something worth keeping.
You throw out the net and haul it back
empty, torn open, filled with the usual
garbage. Nothing surprises you anymore
but the next cast, or the next—
you'll work all night if you have to,
knowing it's probably stupid, it's
probably not the best way to spend your time.
Your wife is anxious, the children
wonder what's happened to their old man,
moody as dark river water.
But you don't do this very often,
you tell yourself—it's a trip you've
put off too long to stop now. And then
there's a small flash of something
tangled hopelessly in the netting.
You can tell it's not what you wanted,
but you keep on working. If there's one,
there will have to be others.

After a few nights of this
you might have something worth keeping
after all—the results of your casting
spread out before you on a table.
Here, you say to your wife, take a look
at this and tell me what you think.
It's good, she says, squinting in
the room's flat light—but then, I

don't know much about nightfishing.
Look at this, you say to your friends,
the ones who know something about nets
and rivers. Unusual but interesting,
one says; another talks of trying
different, stronger nets, like his.

Later, when you're finally at a
stopping place—work's not finished,
just abandoned, as some wise nightfisher
has said—you decide to send out word
of your catch, knowing that no one will
probably notice, not really, anyway.
No matter—the river's high again tonight,
swollen with run-off from a rainy season.
You feel the old tug of the moon,
the net's quicksilver flash into dark water,
disappearing, beyond all promise of return.

Along the Shore

Minnesota Gothic

"It may be that the affection its poets
have for the heartland is the sort a
parent will have for the homelier or
less endowed child."

—Lucien Stryk, from his introduction
to *Heartland: Poets of the Midwest*

Reclining Nude

Minnesota Gothic

—for Bud and Little Bingo

There's a hole in the west-bound lane,
a barricade, a sign: "Take Turns,"
it says. Take turns—or you'll
never get to the Ortonville Cafe
and that slice of "raison" pie.

Bumper stickers read "Norvegian Power,"
and farmers waggle fingers as they pass
in pickup trucks. In the Oasis Bar
the old man in the seed hat wonders
what the crops and girls are like
where I come from—and then we
settle back and watch the "Please—
Do Not Throw Coins at Dancers" sign.

"Take turns," I say. The old man grins
like a Viking. "It's quite the deal,"
he says—and then the night
comes down around us, filled with
dusty roads and shining eyes.

A Mighty Fortress

"On gray days we reflected weather color.
Lutherans did that. It made us children of God."
—Richard Hugo

Maybe it wasn't so bad—
that time I thought everyone
in Minnesota must be Lutheran,
everyone who counted, anyway.
When I remember, there is always
sweat, the dark rooms where we
learned to fear and love God
every Saturday in confirmation class.

It was always cloudy at that church,
where I shoveled walks, lit altar candles,
played ball—whatever it took to be saved.
They said the preacher was a good Norwegian
but we knew he had to be a Russian
to scare the hell out of us like that.
Or into us. He was what we
thought about, every night and day.

Maybe it wasn't so bad—
when I remember, there are hymns
and bells and banquets in the basement,
the eyes of our parents,
stunned, forever fading into sepia.
After all, we were the children of God—
who learned to keep our heads down,
who wondered if we'd ever get away.

Second Service

Old men are dancing tonight in Fargo,
and in a hundred towns in Minnesota
Swede bands are braying polkas to the
       Northern Cross.
Accordions seduce fat women in corners.
Naked clarinets prance and twist behind
       a gauze of smoke.

Children, where are your parents tonight?
The doors to their mead halls are locked
and the darkness grows heavy
with the ceremony of their secret singing.

The Footballers

They still wear high school jerseys,
numbers faded into gray. Along the bar
they shout and pass imaginary balls
and diagram old moves in spilt beer.
Each call relives a certain game—
a conference grudge match or a superbowl,
or years ago in some small town
whose name they can't quite remember—
only that those guys were all pussies.
High fives. Another round.

They leave at closing, one by one,
lugging their bellies through the aisles.
The quarterback sits alone at the bar,
hat akimbo, arms collapsed, waiting
for someone to show him the way home—
out past the streetlights and empty cars,
the fast freights roaring in the stands.

The Lost Viking

Call of the Wild

How we must love our animals,
the visitor remarks—
each town erects a statue
to its totem mallard, beaver,
walleyed pike. We're noted too
for plastic fawns demure among the
birdbaths, trolls, and pinwheels.

See the bear cub in his cage
at the gas station, raccoons
hissing by the Coke machine,
the pacing fox and timber wolf.
Deer Town's just ahead—
feed the deer, pet the deer,
take home another unique souvenir.

How we must love our animals—
driving out to meet them
in our pickup trucks and snowmobiles.
We love their eyes, their shining
eyes in headlights, dear visitor—
our love is boundless as the tall grass,
the dark woods calling, calling.

Dog and Volvo

The Visitor

Some days it's like this—
the house is empty,
getting dark at 5 o'clock.
Soon this page will disappear

and I'll sit here in the kitchen
rocking and listening to the
furnace talk to the refrigerator,
the coffee to the clock.

Now the red light on the stove
makes small eyes in the window.
The wind comes up, a gust of
snowflakes brushes glass.

Some days it's like this—
you come home to find a man
waiting in a dark kitchen
holding his breath.

Snow Dance, Snow Dream

All around us now, spread out like centuries
the prairies fill with snow—
drifts unstoppable, across each fence and boundary.
The small house tilts in reckless winds.

Then, for no good reason, walls have held,
and one by one the snow beasts
come in from the storm, through the long night,
steaming and stamping around the kitchen,
rubbing their backs against ceiling beams,
fanning their wings against black window glass.

By first light, only the tiny fires of their eyes
are still alive—

Still Life with Thermometer

Today you remember windchill—
40, 50, 60 below—
after a point it ceases to matter.
Your car is sealed in ice.
All footprints have drifted over,
houses drawn up together
in a ring of smoke.

How do you speak of the real winter?
It's cold, you say. Cold.
It moves through doors and walls.
This is the way you have learned to speak,
without postmarks, without stamps.

You watch the dead growth
of last summer's garden
rising from the snow,
a spider frozen on the windowsill,
the gathering dark—
your own cloudy breath
bearing messages
to each corner of the room.

Clark Kent

House for Rent

Across the street the porch light burns all night
but no one seems to come or go.
"Someone must live there, don't you think?"
the neighbor woman asks. "I seen a mail truck
stop the other day, but then it blocked my view."

Night after night the porch light burns,
one naked bulb to spark all conversation
on this side of the street. "They must work late,
they must be odd, or don't you think?"
The neighbors watch and wait.

Someday soon there'll be another mail truck,
a bit of snow to sweep from the front steps.
Someday soon the lightbulb will burn out
and then we'll see who dares keep us wondering,
and if it's anyone we'd like to know.

Tubing

North of North

Today with no surprise
the windchill sinks to 50 below.
The mailman slouches up the walk,
head down, the way we all learn how
to walk on this far edge.
You write to say how cold it must be here,
and thank whatever gods you have
this weather's north of you, far north.

But we say it too—
it's always colder somewhere else.
We praise our plows and furnaces,
fall back again on what we know:
there are no last words,
and what we speak of
is neither storm nor chill,
but what would happen if all letters stopped—
that other winter, directionless,
colder than ice, deeper than snow.

Forty Days and Forty Nights

Going Home

"I am driving; it is dusk; Minnesota.
The stubble field catches the last growth of sun.
The soybeans are breathing on all sides."

—Robert Bly, from "Driving toward the
Lac Qui Parle River"

Heritage Home

Two Rivers

"I thought it would be bigger"
is what visitors always say. "Is this
the same Red River in the song?"
This stubborn, sluggish, silty stream
that loops its way the wrong direction,
north—it doesn't even burn,
the way that some polluted rivers do.
Perhaps we need to make it burn.

Not far from here the Mississippi
starts its long amble to the Gulf.
"Now *there's* a river," tourists say;
"we walked across the source near
Lake Itasca once," holding up that
pleasant country creek the way
they'd hold up the snapshot of a fish—
proud possessors of another myth.

Their minds are full of steamboats,
barges, sprawling river towns with accents
dimly strange. There's no talking to
people like that. "Germs," we say;
"they've found them here in record numbers,
even malaria. And chemicals"—
remembering the year the awful beet plant
stench moved downriver from the south.

"Just think," the tourists say,
"the mighty Mississippi starts
only about a hundred miles away"—
the stuff of faith and pilgrimage.
Here, the Red is simply backwards, serpentine,
and darkly grim, the stuff of lesser dreams,
the source of something harder to define—
beyond burning, closer to home.

The First Days of Summer

The children hurry home to swell the house
with plans. What will they ever do
to fill their time, I say—remembering
my own long lists of unread summer books,

the calendars I saved for checking off
triumphant days away from school,
each square filled with nothing
but brilliant sun and a dark blue X.

Tomorrow I'll put in the garden,
or the day after, if it doesn't rain.
Perhaps by August we can get away,
if the car holds up, if the house gets painted.

Upstairs, the children argue over records.
A sudden breeze bends weeds and dandelions.
Somewhere a great blue heron soars,
and lake waves lap against a dock.

Weeds thicken, paint peels. I turn
another page, unsure of what I've read:
time to check the lists and calendars again,
the empty sidewalks filling up with sun.

Dog, Cooling

Red River Blues

Tonight the news of drought
sweeps in on western winds—
topsoil laced with smoke and snow.
Nothing can stop that message here.

The empty rain gauge chants
the last faint summer dreams;
around the house the earth
has sunk another inch this week.

Even flat land falls away: this is
the place where all directions cease.
Just past town is the only hill—
the overpass for the Interstate.

Always a Wind

—for Ted Kooser

Today it's August on the Interstate—
snowfences rolled and stacked
beside the disappearing, dusty brown.
Our rivers leak away like salt.
Our summer hunger leans against the clouds.

But even in the evening's calm
there's always a wind, restless and unstoppable.
Take nothing for granted, it seems to say—
especially not those flat, familiar miles
you think you see beyond.

Sod

Cultured Sod

Urban Renewal

Two blocks away, I see the
dust cloud rising above trees,
and then the small frame house
I've walked by every day for years—
the claw of the steam shovel
rises up behind the roof,
tears its way back to the chimney.

It's not called a claw, not
called a steam shovel—I know that—
but in a world turned empty as a
movie set, one stands and gapes—
with mothers and their clapping kids,
with french fry munchers from
McDonald's just down the street.

One stands and gapes and passes by.
Tomorrow, the rubble will be gone,
the hole filled in, new sod laid down.
It's just an old house—I know that,
numbed by the clang of dump trucks
lining up like giant sandbox toys.
Besides, they're waiting supper
just a few more blocks from here—
the small frame house that I
come home to every day.

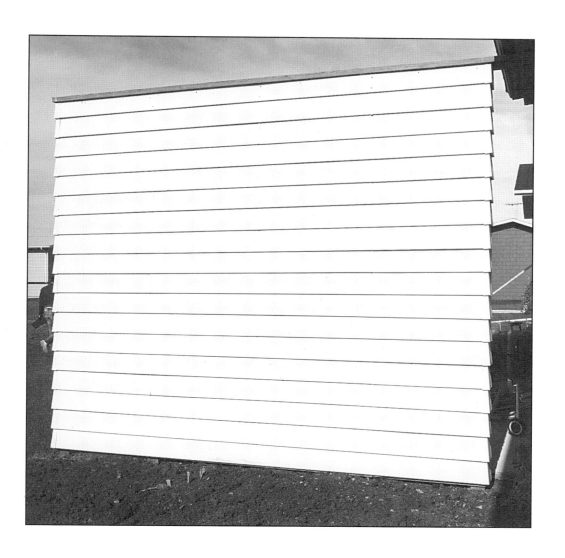

White Wall

Auction Sale

—for Rosemary and George Smith

You have to have a number
if you want to bid.
Don't mind the leering, empty house—
these sawhorse tables on the lawn
hold bargains, friends,
and we always save the best for last.

In and out the bidders swim,
nudging lacework, dishes, books.
Atop his pickup truck the auctioneer
begins to cluck into his microphone:
a dollar here and then six bits,
who'll make it two or four or ten?
The grinning fat man holds up
fishing poles. "That fool,"
the woman in the pink suit says.
Her husband's bought another lamp.

The crowd is growing now
and kids with ice cream cones
have found the TV sets.
"Whose sale is this?" ask women
trying all the suitcase locks.
"My grandson is a golfer,
so he'll like these clubs"—
the old man's pride is written on
the pile he's stashed beside the curb.

"Whose sale is this?" they ask,
and most are holding something new—
a piece of someone else's life
to graft onto their own,
if the price is right
and spouses hold their tongues.
You have to have a number
if you want to bid—
they move in tightening circles now,
knowing that the best is always
saved until the end.

In a Drought Year

—for Joe Richardson

The barn was empty,
falling down,
the windmill bent
like a discarded paper hat.
We passed a hundred like it—
talked of mountains, surf,
anything to keep us from
the heat and dying corn—
until we stopped
to watch an orange moon rise
and string our breaths
across those cooling fields—
going nowhere,
but going home.

Homesteaders

—for Brom Griffin

When they came
some of them already knew
that here was more than flatness;
here at last was a place
where all things would be possible.

* *

Call it ocean, call it desert;
trails move off in all directions—
tall grass, wheat field, open range.
Everyone here is traveler.
No one knows the way.

* *

The buffalo wallow is thick with prairie aster,
coneflower, gentian, blazing star.
We walk the fields till dusk,
when deer come down to drink at the river
and a cool wind ruffles the bluestem.
The sky is full of old bones.

Big Sky

Autumn Songs

1.

The elm tree points a
bare branch at my window.
For the ten-thousandth time
in this life
I pull on my socks.

2.

Tractor parked in the middle
of a half-plowed field,
farmer gathering bittersweet
in the woodlot, shotguns
bellowing beyond a haze of sumac.

3.

Wet roads covered with salamanders—
sluggish executives going nowhere.
We fish into dusk
catching only leaves in the water.

4.

All the way home
only the full moon
is drunker than we are,
rising on each gust—
cargo of smoke and sleep.

About the poet

Mark Vinz was born in Rugby, North Dakota, grew up in Minneapolis and the Kansas City area, attended the Universities of Kansas and New Mexico, and since 1968 has taught at Moorhead State University in Minnesota, where he is currently a professor of English; he is also the editor of Dacotah Territory Press.

His poems have been published in several magazines and anthologies, in six chapbook collections, and in two full-length collections: *Climbing the Stairs* and *Mixed Blessings* (both published by Spoon River Poetry Press). He is also the author of two books of prose poems, *The Weird Kid* and *Late Night Calls* (both published by New Rivers Press); co-editor with Thom Tammaro of *Common Ground: A Gathering of Poems on Rural Life* and an anthology of Midwestern literature (to be published by the University of Minnesota Press in 1993), and he is co-editor with Dave Williamson of *Beyond Borders: New Writing from Manitoba, Minnesota, Saskatchewan and the Dakotas.* Several of his short stories have appeared in magazines, and in newspapers via five PEN Syndicated Fiction Project awards.

He lives with his wife Betsy in Moorhead; their two daughters Katie and Sarah are attending graduate schools in Kansas and New York.

About the photographer

Wayne Gudmundson lives in Moorhead, Minnesota, with his wife Jane and daughter Liv. They share their house with the two wondercats Walt and Tuna. In addition to various exhibits, his work has appeared in the following books: *Oil: Photographs from the Williston Basin* (ACME Invisible Inc., 1982), *Iron Spirits* (North Dakota Council on the Arts, 1982), *A Long Way to See: Images and Voices of North Dakota* (The Institute for Regional Studies, North Dakota State University, 1987), and *Testaments in Wood: Finnish Log Structures at Embarrass, Minnesota* (Minnesota Historical Society, 1991).

His work is in the collections of The Museum of Modern Art, New York; The PaineWebber Collection, New York; Centre Canadien d'Architecture, Montreal, Canada; Minnesota Historical Society, St. Paul; and others, including Ralph's Bar in Moorhead, Minnesota.

Gudmundson presently teaches photography in the Department of Mass Communications at Moorhead State University, Moorhead, Minnesota.

Dead End

Titling in Goudy Bold Italic
and text in Goudy Old Style
typeset by Jodee Kulp Graphic Arts.
Printed on acid-free Mountie Matte
by Friesen Printers.

Special thanks
to Peter Lindman
for his hand coloring
of the cover photograph.